MW01228556

Printed in the United States of America
ISBN Paperback 9798865326021

Early Praise for *Collaborating in Competitive Ecosystems*

This book has been such a joy to read. Ashley has been able to connect with us with the many characters she has portrayed in the book. The topics she talks about are something that most women deal with. Being able to share the things women go through in her book helps us realize that it's all part of the process and we can rise up from it to be leaders in our own right. Thank you, Ashley, your book will inspire so many!

~ Sheena Yap Chan, Author of *the WSJ Bestselling work, The Tao of Self-Confidence: A Guide to Moving Beyond Trauma and Awakening the Leader Within* by Wiley (2023)

In *Collaborating in Competitive Ecosystems*, you'll meet a cast of personable characters who navigate the complex terrain of leadership with humor and heart. Through a series of Micro-Learning Moments, this story imparts upon readers invaluable lessons and profound wisdom, providing essential tools to cultivate a strong leadership mindset essential in any business environment.

~ Nicole Cohen, UCLA Graduate 2023 and (Nico, the Tree Frog) Litigation Assistant, VPG

In *Collaborating in Competitive Ecosystems*, readers find essential leadership lessons tailored for those working in a multicultural environment, making it an ideal training tool for children and adults.

~ US Ambassador Lisa Gable, WSJ & USA Today Best-Selling Author of *Turnaround: How to Change Course When Things Are Going South* by Ideapress Publishing (2021)

Refreshingly truthful and completely lovable. Ashley's book captures the essence of both her personality and the American office culture. In an era where young professionals crave guidance, this unique read offers invaluable mentorship, teaching you how to shine authentically while respecting others.

~ Janet Bruins, writer + mother, Bechtel's Financial Systems Manager

The author offers readers an inspiring and insightful journey through the world of entrepreneurship. Her mission is clear: to impart the invaluable lessons she has gathered along the way. Her emphasis on diversity, equity, inclusion, and accessibility (DEIA) is a breath of fresh air, and she presents these critical themes through the engaging lens of the VPG team's animal characters. Through their stories, the book provides a unique and illuminating perspective on leadership dynamics within contemporary workplaces. It's an exploration of experiences, both positive and challenging, that contribute to not only individual growth but also the collective advancement within our ecosystems. The author's unwavering belief that understanding one's purpose and "WHY" is the key to navigating the demanding terrain of leadership shines through, providing readers with a compelling guide to cultivating success in both personal and professional spheres.

~ Shawnna Hoffman, President, Guardrail Technologies and Responsible AI Blockchain & Cybersecurity Subject Matter Expert

Table of Contents

Dedication – To My Family

Credit: Violii

You are never too small to make a difference.

- Greta Thunberg, environmental activist

Foreword

Collaborating in Competitive Ecosystems marks a deliberate shift from my earlier work, *Building a Leadership Habitat.* In my initial work, I explored personal growth and professional identity, often grappling with imposter syndrome.

As a business owner and a Woman of Color (WOC), specifically Asian American, my goal is to share the lessons I've learned on my entrepreneurial journey. I aim to emphasize diversity, equity, inclusion, and accessibility (DEIA) through the stories of the VPG team's animal characters, offering a unique perspective on leadership dynamics in today's workplaces. These experiences, both positive and challenging, contribute to individual and collective growth within our ecosystems.

I aspire to turn this work into a practical guidebook, fostering an environment where leaders and team members feel safe to speak up and collaborate toward common goals, drawing inspiration from the animals in our PeTab Village ecosystems. Throughout the ten chapters of this illustrated book, I also explore the power of mindset and reframing limiting beliefs, through our animal characters' voices.

My journey started with the pursuit of work-life balance after years in a demanding litigation field. I am deeply grateful for the experience gained during those years and the qualities it instilled in me. I appreciate the support of the VPG network and encourage others to pursue their dreams.

This work distinguishes itself by documenting the transition from a "me" to a "we" mindset, inspired by authors like Deepa Purushothaman in *The First, The Few, The Only,* Anna Yusim, M.D. *Fulfilled: How the Science of Spirituality Can Help You Live a Happier, More Meaningful Life,* and Sheena Yap Chan, *The Tao of Self-Confidence: A Guide to Moving Beyond Trauma and Awakening the Leader Within.* While we strive for personal growth, we also recognize our interconnectedness within our ecosystems and aim to foster collaborative communities.

As a solopreneur, relinquishing control and admitting mistakes have been challenging. Overcoming cultural pressures to maintain a flawless image remains a work in progress.

Collaborating with Michelle Kim, our illustrator, has been both challenging and rewarding. We have worked together to depict lessons through illustrations and created "Micro-learning Moments" (MLMs) inspired by my Olympian Skeleton friend Jane Channel. During my visit to Calgary, Jane offered me her hipster approach of this MLM acronym, not to be confused with the "Multi-Level Marketing" method. In this book, MLM refers to a bite-sized learning module, our five key takeaways at the end of each chapter.

The theme of women empowerment is central to this book, drawing on DEIA lessons shared by guests from VPG's "Virtual Water Cooler Chat" Podcast. These lessons include self-acceptance, boundary setting, aligning words and actions, and confidence building.

Starting a podcast on women's empowerment in 2023 has been unexpectedly fulfilling, allowing us to hear the voices of successful women in various industries through this virtual platform. Despite progress, gender biases persist in male-dominated fields at C-Suites levels, as well as in law and medicine. Through storytelling, I hope to inspire and support each other's growth.

Entrepreneurship may not be for everyone, however, for those choosing to stay within organizations, practicing intra-entrepreneurship can be fruitful. Leadership is a demanding endeavor and understanding one's purpose and "WHY" can lead to a personal and professional fulfillment. Moreover, I hope to devote this book to those who care about fostering understanding between generational workforce and helping make our future bright.

With a collaborative and growth-focused mindset, let's embark on this journey together!

Acknowledgment

Hvala　谢谢　Gracias　Danke

감사합니다　Bedankt

ありがとう

Salamat　Merci

Kiitos　Thank you　شکریہ

Cảm ơn　Grazie

(mk) Sep. 2023

I am deeply grateful to the Virtual Patent Gateway (VPG) team for their unwavering support and shared vision. I especially enjoy the process of growing together with our resident illustrator, Michelle Kim. Through challenges, I have learned that positivity inspires valuable learning experiences. As our team evolves, some members explore new careers, and others may no longer align, but the time spent together is critical for learning.

The VPG team provided character descriptions, and I appreciate those who helped me in this treacherous editing process, including the beta readers who provided wonderful feedback. This journey has reinforced that leadership is about influence, not titles. There's no crystal ball, but we grow through heartfelt conversations with our team. Credit goes to the team for successes, and leaders must hold people, including themselves, accountable when things go wrong.

I want to express my heartfelt appreciation to my mother, Cheungma, and to my brothers, Eric and Ken, for their steadfast support. Since Dad's passing, they have become the cornerstone of my life. My extended family is also invaluable in helping me learn and grow, their support means the world to me. I extend my gratitude to friends who have stood by me: Shana Cyr, Michael Loulakis, Kelly Boudreau, Jon Stroud, Melanie Grover, Meredith Schoenfeld, Sara Cooksey, Wanshan Wang, Kara Specht, Jess Marks, Angela Evans, Michele Vineyard, Jessica McLean, Jane Channell, Brendan Hines-Ike, Jan Pearson Srock, Michele Vineyard, Sheena Yap Chan, Heather Martin, Nicole Cohen, and Natasha Durkins. Your presence in my life has been a source of strength and warmth.

I owe an immeasurable debt of gratitude to my clients and mentors, among them the late Clyde Stoltenberg, who profoundly shaped my values as an immigrant daughter who struggled to find my place at the university. Sasha Strauss, your exemplary blend of spirit, brilliance, and kindness has been a guiding light. Mark Green, you have served as a no-nonsense coach, encouraging candidness. Kristen Hadeed, your mentorship in delivering critical feedback and fearlessly owning our mistakes as leaders has been transformative. These are humbling lessons that are vital to impart to the next generation of leaders as they step into positions of leadership, while staying true to themselves.

Lastly, to the readers embarking on this journey, your interest is the ultimate reward. As a non-attorney practitioner in the PTAB space, I offer unique perspectives to bridge gaps in the legal industry. I hope this book provides you with value and inspiration.

Chapter 1
To Trust or Not to Trust, That is the Question!

Xǐlè does not always trust others as she has been burned so many times before. Now that there are new inhabitants with different experiences, backgrounds, and outlooks in the habitat, she knows that she will have to rely more on her core team to help lead the rest. She does have an internal conflict that she must reconcile. Her heart tells her she needs to trust others until they are proven otherwise; however, her head, based on her past negative experiences, is having a difficult time letting go of that control and getting hurt. Xǐlè decides to just go with the flow and allow her heart to guide her to help integrate the

PeTab Ecosystem with this new hybrid ecosystem. She knows that it will be challenging, but she thinks the lessons learned will be worthwhile. She has observed some key traits of both the original and the new inhabitants that concern her, so she decides to call a kick-off meeting with an additional six residents to help her brainstorm: Sarang (Chief People Officer), Paprika (Webinar and Podcast Producer), Hanso (Project Analyst), Alexandra (Digital Strategist), Toto (Illustrator/Junior Artistic Analyst) and Chika (Junior Project Engineer).

Xǐlè's goal is to gain new, unbiased perspectives, so she purposefully selects the quiet members of the original inhabitants and new members. There will be other chances for town hall meetings that allow everyone to voice their concerns, but she wants a smaller group and encourages participation first. She meditates on how she could make everything into a collaboration instead of a conflict.

Xǐlè decides to hold a breakfast meeting near the waterfall outside of the PeTab ecosystem. She has Sara and Luminary set up the breakfast area and explains to them why they are not included in this breakfast meeting. She does not want them to misunderstand, and she wants this communicated straight from the owl's mouth! That's how trust is built, through respect and direct communication, not through the grapevines!

As the meeting attendees join, Xǐlè greets each one. When everyone arrives, Xǐlè welcomes them, "Welcome all, and thank you for getting up bright and early to join us with this kick-off meeting. Let's start by having each of you introduce yourself in this order: Sarang, Paprika, Hanso, Alexandra, Toto, and Chika. Any objections?" Everyone nods.

"Hello, I am Sarang, I am the Chief People Officer (CPO), the impala. I have known Xǐlè for over two decades and we used to work together. I really want to support the PeTab Ecosystem as I think this is a worthwhile goal and I hope to make a difference. I love people, but I am more of a follower than a leader. I don't mind learning, though."

"Morning, I am Paprika, the black leopard. I am a vocalist and I like to mind my own business and do my own things. I have other projects going on, so I like to be left alone to do my thing. I have known Xǐlè and the PeTab Ecosystem for over two years. I think the world needs a positive change, and I want to help Xǐlè spread the message through our innovative webinars and podcast that touches others' hearts."

"I am Hanso. I am a meerkat. I learned about PeTab Ecosystem and got to know Xǐlè during a very brief time. I am a transient member of this community, but while I am here, I don't mind helping. I love solving problems and I want to build a community of my own, so this is a good experience for me. I will be leaving the ecosystem, but Xǐlè said that she still wants my opinion. So here I am."

"Hi, I am Alexandra, the lion. I am a big fan of the ecosystem and I love my meeting with Xǐlè. I feel accepted as who I am; although, Xǐlè can be quite candid when she provides feedback. I enjoyed the fact that she does not use the "compliment sandwich" technique, so I feel that her feedback is for my own growth. I am the digital strategist and I want to work with our team to expand the message of our ecosystem, just like Paprika."

"Umm, I am Toto, the zebra. I am an illustrator and the youngest member of the ecosystem. I like to draw and Xǐlè offered me many opportunities to draw and grow. I don't like to speak a lot, but I am here to help."

"Hello, I am Chika, the leopard. I have known Xǐlè since I was little, but we were not close. When the drought happened and we all had to move to PeTab

Ecosystem, I got a chance to observe everyone, and I truly enjoyed the camaraderie that everyone brought to the table. I am a science kind of gal, and I don't want to miss a beat, so I'm here to help. Just show me the way."

Xǐlè smiles and thanks everyone. She also explains the concept of a compliment sandwich, where you start with a compliment, then your real message (usually critical feedback that may not be positive), and then add another compliment. She wants to set the expectation with this group that she prefers not to tiptoe with everyone, but she recognizes that she has to earn everyone's trust first. Then, she asks everyone to have their breakfast and get to know each other.

After breakfast, Xǐlè restarts the meeting and announced the goals of the meeting. "We want to hear each one of your inputs so we can have a seamless integration of our growing ecosystem," Xǐlè says.

"I agree," Sarang nods and speaks. "Peanut (the giraffe) won a national competition and will be moving away soon, but she wants to stay on as she can, and works with us as a consultant. We need someone to be trained to learn some of the current tasks she handles.

Maybe Roo could take over for her. If we transition now, then Peanut can offer insight and training," Sarang suggests.

Xǐlè says, "Roo (the fast black cat) is very energetic, and she has a kind heart, but she has a full schedule with her other job."

Sarang repeats to herself out loud, "Henrietta left to be a writer. Maybe Sara could take on that responsibility. I know she has a lot of duties with protecting the ecosystem, but I believe she enjoys writing and this would give her some time to do something she loves." Xǐlè indicates, "Sara can certainly help, and

4

we can check with her, but I think that may be overwhelming. I like the fact that you are already observing different personalities of our ecosystem, and I guess that's why we made you the CPO."

"Toto and Luminary would work well together if we are encouraging collaboration. They are both artistic but have different strengths that would mesh well together," Sarang suggests.

"That would be a positive pairing," Xǐlè agrees.

"What are we going to do about Scar, the hyena?" Toto asks. "We have never interacted with someone with that taker personality, and I don't have a good vibe about him." Xǐlè is surprised and impressed that Toto speaks up.

"I will keep an eye on Scar, but I think everyone deserves a fair chance. We don't know what Scar may have experienced that led him to behave so selfishly. I have always said that everyone is selfish to a certain extent, so we will have to take this as we come." Xǐlè says, looking perplexed.

"That will be difficult, but I know that you got this," Chika states with confidence. Xǐlè says, "Yes, we got this!"

"I think it would also be a good idea for Misha (the tiger) and Keola (the pangolin) to work together. They are both coaches and are good at reading people. My senses tell me that they will be a strong team," Alexandra says.

"Woodbury would be a good person to assist with projects that need attention to detail. He is meticulous and when we need something that requires precision, he can be called in," Paprika says.

"Luna can fly around and make sure that everything is running smoothly. I know that Sara patrols and we have the drone, but it is great to have another pair of eyes now that we have a growing community. Having a collaborative community is one of my top priorities for the PeTab Ecosystem to grow and continue to be successful. I am so happy to learn new insights from all of you this morning. I will chat with Sara and Luminary, and we will have our next Pow Wow meeting. Until then, I would like each of you to write down five ideas you have to help grow our ecosystem, anything goes, put them in an envelope and do not put your name, put them in the ecosystem's suggestion box by next Monday, we will announce those suggestions in the next ecosystem meeting. Sounds good?"

"We got this!" Sarang and others all respond enthusiastically.

Xǐlè smiles, "We are here to complete each other and not compete with each other, according to the leadership guru, John Maxwell. Now that we have our first meeting, let's figure out how to help each of our inhabitants grow while growing our ecosystem."

MLM* = Micro-Learning Moments

1. Trust your team but maintain your voice as a leader.

2. Delegation is important as a leader as it helps grow your team. Depending on the relationship, you want to trust but verify as you are ultimately responsible for the outcome as a leader. Guide your team through delegation and convert them into high performers.

3. Give your team a chance to grow and prove themselves. Focus on the positive lessons learned rather than perceived failures.

4. Gather support for yourself as a leader, both from your team and also from outside sources.

5. Accept input from your team, but help them understand that, as leader, you may make final decisions that may be unpopular. Once final decisions are made, your team needs to respect and support your role as leader.

Chapter 2
On Toxicity and Scarcity

Xǐlè feels grounded after her meditation. She reviews her journal and now it is the time for her to discuss her thoughts with Sara and Luminary. Xǐlè asks Sara to reserve the community room so the three of them can meet. At the last minute, Xǐlè invites Hetter, the Fennec Fox to join and observe.

"So how did everything go yesterday with your meeting without us?" Sara is eager to learn the juicy details.

"It was interesting, and I think we have our hands full," Xǐlè smiles.

"What do you mean?" Luminary asks with curiosity.

"Our ecosystem is scaling and there will be new personalities and ideas that may not mesh well with the original collaborative culture we have tried to build, and I already noticed some negative vibes. I am just not so sure how best to navigate the water yet." Xĭlè looks perplexed, but she wants to be honest with Sara and Luminary. She adds, "Everyone seems to have a positive attitude except for Scar. He makes many sly remarks and even Toto observes the toxicity in his attitude. Toto generally does not judge but she's very observant. She's our youngest member here. To some extent, we want to protect her. However, I also think Toto should learn lessons on her own. That is a part of growth, right?"

"Hetter, what do you think? Should we protect Toto or have her learn her lesson on her own?" Sara asks.

Hetter, being a newcomer, feels like she is put on the spot. She asks Sara, "What was the question again?"

"Can you be more specific about what makes Scar's attitudes toxic?" Luminary interjected as she sensed Hetter's hesitance and wanted to help.

"Sure, here at the PeTab Ecosystem, we all work together. It is critical to the continued success of our ecosystem. It's just my instinct for now. I found Scar covering his mouth a lot when he did not get his way. Scar also put Toto and Chika down and ran them down like a steamroller. I don't like that." Xĭlè knows that her instinct is correct, but she also wants to be fair and balanced between being overprotective and allowing Toto and Chika to learn their life lessons.

At this time, there is a loud knock on the community room door. Xǐlè states, "Yes, please enter." It is Timo. Xǐlè invites Timo to join this meeting as she values his opinion, and she knows that Timo has known Scar for much longer than anyone has in the ecosystem.

"Hello, everyone, something came up and I am sorry I am late to the meeting. When Xǐlè asked me to join, I did warn her that I am busy at the golf course, as it is a busy season. However, I made it as Xǐlè and I are good friends and I want to support her in whatever way I can," Timo says.

"Timo, we really appreciate you taking the time out of your day to meet and the reason for this meeting is to discuss Scar, as we have some concerns about Scar's behavior and we want to protect our team, while also allowing each member of our ecosystem to learn lessons on their own. We thought we would talk to you and see if you have any recommendations on how best to accomplish that goal," Xǐlè says. Timo knows immediately Xǐlè's intention and starts to say, "Umm, I see. Perhaps a story will help, and you may draw your own conclusion. Sounds good?"

"A few months ago, my golf course was trashed, and we could not figure out for the longest time who the culprit was. I got together with our team, and Scar was one of our team members. During various meetings, Scar would roll his eyes but not say anything. I advised Scar and the others, and their first assignment was to figure out who was trashing the ecosystem. It was obviously the hyenas, but we did not have any evidence until we reviewed the surveillance footage. We also knew that Scar was not going to tell on his packs.

Long story short, I gave at least three opportunities for Scar to confess. Each time, Scar would say he knew nothing. It was not until I showed him irrefutable video evidence that he pleaded, 'I am sorry, I just could not tell on my friends even when I knew they were wrong.'" Timo still appears annoyed when he repeats the story.

Sara says with anger, "I knew it! You should not tolerate a liar and toxic behaviors. They don't change and they will only taint your community and suck out all the positive vibes. I am curious, though, how did you handle this situation? And was Scar kicked out of your team?"

Timo says, "I wish it would be that easy. I must admit that I sometimes give in when I don't want to. I am not very good about confronting bad behaviors. I wish I could be more candid, so that's an area that I need to grow in."

Luminary asks, "What is Scar afraid of? I know it is not cool to tell on friends, but if they are wrong, I think we have a duty to help them. Telling the truth is important in this instance."

Timo says, "I think Scar exhibits malicious qualities because he is afraid of not being accepted by his pack. He really wants to be accepted and deep down, he may be more insecure than we think he is. Sometimes, insecurity may be disguised as a grandiose ego. It's one way to cover up their own faults. So, I decided to give him another chance but noted that potential quality of his."

"We cannot trust him. That is his nature. He is toxic, you know!" Sara insists.

Luminary asks, "Xĭlè, what do you think?"

"We will keep an eye on Scar. While I wish life was so easy that we could just exclude anyone negative or with a scarcity mindset so we could all be happy and trust one another, it is not always realistic. Hurt people *hurt* people, you know," Xĭlè says and Timo nods.

"What is scarcity mindset?" Sara and Luminary both ask simultaneously.

"A scarcity mindset is generally negative and focuses on what is missing instead of what may be gained. Look at it this way, it is a zero-sum game mentality. If there is an apple pie, people with a scarcity mentality would think that they need to have more slices, and having others join would cause them to lose another slice," Xǐlè says, "Make sense?"

Luminary asks, "Why can't they think of baking more apple pies?"

Xǐlè and Timo both laugh, "I am so happy you are learning here. What you stated is the opposite of the scarcity mindset — the abundance mindset. This is why mindset is so important and helps determine why someone behaves the way they do."

Sara nods, "We have our hands full for sure. There's so much to learn and we really appreciate you and Timo taking the time to have this private meeting with us."

"You are team players and will be an asset here for everyone," Xǐlè says in appreciation.

"In the future, you both will probably be paired with Scar, you now have some new insights about him and know how to work with him and protect others, when needed. The others will learn eventually, and that's just part of growth," Xǐlè says.

"It is great to be appreciated for specific skills. You are lucky as Xǐlè has experienced a lot and she is kind," Timo says.

Xǐlè says, "I am happy to share my experience and I will not shy away from problems and be super candid if I have to. But I think we should give others a chance to prove themselves first. On that note, we should all return to our duties."

Timo says, "Agreed, I better return to the golf course and see what is in store for me today. Don't hesitate to let me know if you all need to pick my brain. I am at your disposal."

Luminary and Sara say, "Yes, Timo. We really do appreciate having you join our meeting today. We learned so much! Have a great day."

MLM* = Micro-Learning Moments

1. Be kind to others, you never know what they are going through.

2. Give others a chance, however, hold people accountable for their behaviors. That's where growth happens.

3. Healthy competition is good for a workplace but be careful of rewarding toxic high performers. Toxic high performers are the ones that deliver outcomes at all costs.

4. Encourage collaboration among your team – Collaboration breeds new ideas and positive energy.

5. When you are a leader, you WILL be judged. Be the leader that your team can come to when things go wrong by having the courage to admit when you are incorrect and accepting responsibility.

Chapter 3
On People Pleasing

Xǐlè gives Sara the task of painting the PeTab Ecosystem sign. It desperately needs updating and she wants Sara to oversee the project.

"Sara, our sign needs painting and I want you to oversee this project. However, I want you to involve other members of our growing ecosystem. I like you to delegate with minimal frustration on your part," Xǐlè says to Sara during their morning meeting.

"I will gladly accept this task. Do you have anyone specific in mind?" Sara asks.

"Hmm, I like to take this opportunity to help some of our residents to reflect on their own people-pleasing attitude and learn to work as a team. Any suggestions, based on your observation lately?" Xǐlè asks.

"I think that Woodbury, Chika, Toto, and Sarang would make a good team for this task. What do you think?" Sara curiously asks, hoping that Xǐlè will agree with her.

Xǐlè ponders for a moment. Then she responds, "I think you should decide and take ownership of this project. I prefer not to provide any additional comments, as I think this is also something you would need to learn. I am here to provide feedback. Ask away and I will offer opinions but not until this project is underway."

"With that, Sara, you have autonomy, and the goal is to have the sign painted before our next quarterly meeting. That's the only specification I like to place on this project, for my own planning purposes," Xǐlè says.

Sara is excited and she wants Xǐlè to be proud of her, she immediately goes to talk to everyone. She wants to get this project completed as quickly as possible so she can get back to patrolling the ecosystem, a task that she takes very seriously.

In the interest of saving time, she called a virtual meeting with everyone she had picked while getting paint supplies. As the meeting starts, Sara advises everyone on the goal of the meeting and what they need to accomplish by the next meeting.

"Chika, would you assist me with painting the ecosystem sign? It really needs updating," Sara inquires.

"Sure, I am happy to help," Chika responds quickly.

"Could you meet in a couple of hours to go over what needs to be done?" Sara asks.

"Sure, I will meet you at the sign," Sara says.

Next up is Woodbury. Sara thinks about how easy that had been with Chika. She is patting herself on the back for her excellent leadership skills, and she thinks this will be a cakewalk.

"Woodbury, would you like to help us paint the sign for the ecosystem?" Sara asks.

"I can but it will have to be later," he answers.

"How much later? Chika and I are going to meet in a couple of hours," Sara asks with agitation.

"I am not available but maybe later," Woodbury says ending the conversation.

"I guess Chika and I can meet and come up with a plan," Sara mumbles.

"Send me an email," Woodbury says.

Sara sighs; she really wants to make plans soon, as deep down, she would really like Xǐlè and others to notice that she is leadership material. Sara now realizes that leadership is not so easy because everyone has a mind of their own, and sometimes, they say no. What should she do when people say no?

Toto is up next, and Sara asks if she could meet and assist.

Toto is silent for a moment. "I cannot meet now, but I can try later as I have to meet with Luminary," Toto answers.

"Can't you reschedule? Xǐlè wants us to paint the sign and I need help and we already have a few residents not willing to commit," Sara tries to persuade Toto.

"I wish I could, but I promised Luminary, and I need to keep my promise to her first. I promise I will help, but I just cannot drop everything because you say this takes priority. If you talk to Luminary and she agrees with you, then I may be able to switch my priority and provide you with a definite response. I just can't right now," Toto explains.

"I guess that makes sense. OK. Sarang, what about you?" Sara mumbles again.

Sarang says yes without hesitation. She's the Chief People Officer of the ecosystem and she also does not want to disappoint Xǐlè. Sarang realizes that she has a lot on her plate already, but she wants everyone to be happy, even at her own expense sometimes. Sarang is a giver for sure.

Sara is getting frustrated that not all can commit. She is finding it time-consuming to get everyone's buy-in to get this project done. Everyone has a lot to do. She decides to walk off and revisit it later before she becomes angry.

She runs into Luminary and asks if she can have Toto's help and if they can reschedule the art project. Luminary says without hesitation, "No worries. I can let Toto know that we can reschedule, or would you rather let her know we had this discussion..." Before Luminary finishes her sentence, Sara says, "I will do that. Time is money, you know."

By this time, Woodbury has responded to Sara's email and indicates that after he finished looking at his schedule, he can make it after all. Sara is elated that everything seems to have come together. It is not as easy as she thought it would be.

Sara calls another meeting to go over logistics. She delegates jobs to Chika and Sarang. Chika has a positive attitude and Sarang writes down her assignment and agrees to do her part.

Sara also discusses things that Woodbury could do. She always liked Toto, but she now has a newfound respect for the youngest member of this growing ecosystem.

Sara sent Woodbury his assignments and when she would need them completed. She also emails Chika and Sarang to confirm their assignments. She gives everyone four days to have their part completed.

Sara is ecstatic at the end of the four days that everyone did their part, and the sign is perfect. Sara goes to Xǐlè and says, "We did it and with a few days to spare!"

Xǐlè smiles, "I am glad! And what lessons did you learn here, if any?"

"Well, I learned that being a leader is not easy. Frankly, I did not want you to think I am a bad leader, and there were a few times I may have blown my top when Woodbury and Toto were non-committal. Chika and Sarang were much easier, as they said yes without hesitation. They are true team players, you know," Sara says thinking Xǐlè would agree.

Xǐlè pauses, then says, "I would like to offer a different perspective. I think they are all team players. Woodbury did not say yes immediately as he is working on juggling his projects and boundaries issues. Toto said no because she gave her words to Luminary, and she wants to honor her words. That is integrity. Chika and Sarang will always say yes as they both have some people-pleasing tendencies and, honestly, I do too. We are all a work in progress, you know. Sometimes, it is better to say NO when we know we cannot commit to something. It is being honest about what we can do under the circumstances. Regardless, I think you did a great job in organizing and delegating and I am very proud of you. Thank you, Sara."

Sara smiles and rhetorically asks, "I guess we all have a lot to learn and a lot of space to grow, don't we?"

Xǐlè agrees and is happy to witness Sara's growth.

MLM* = Micro-Learning Moments

1. Remind your team that "NO" is a valid answer, and it is a complete sentence.

2. Focus on growth and managing people-please tendencies.

3. Carve out time for self-care. You cannot grow others when you are running empty yourself.

4. As a leader, you do not have to be doing everything. Find opportunities to delegate to your team and let them shine.

5. Choose being respected instead of being liked. That is the next level of leadership.

Chapter 4
Honor Your Agreements

It is monsoon season and the residents within the PeTab ecosystem need to get ready to protect their home. Xǐlè recalls that the ecosystem suffered a great deal from significant damages. Xǐlè also realizes that she really needs to rely on her core team to help handle the tasks. Streamlining and delegating tasks are the key. She is fearful initially, but she knows it is all or nothing. She knows that her core team will shine if she sets high expectations and is clear about the guidelines. Well, there may be miscommunication from time to time, but she trusts that they will not disappoint her.

Xǐlè, unlike the other owls, is an early riser. She believes in the saying, "early bird gets the worms." That's her parents' teaching. They worked really hard and Xǐlè witnessed both the growth and agony they experienced as they immigrated to PeTab ecosystem. Today, Xǐlè has her daily huddle with Sara and Misha, and she includes Sarang as well. Luminary has an art exhibition that is dear to her heart, so she discusses it with the team, and Xǐlè and Sara will cover for Luminary, with the help of Misha and Sarang. It is so important for Xǐlè to see everyone feel fulfilled during their time in the ecosystem.

"Hello, everyone! Let's start with our huddle today. We have so much to discuss as the monsoon season is approaching," Xǐlè joyfully says while she hands everyone the agenda.

"This is my first real huddle with all of you. I will do what you all need me to do, but I do have some prior appointments. I can mostly meet in the evening and not quite an early owl, hehe," Sarang states meekly.

"Yes, I am here to help too, and I will certainly help everyone channel positive energy and reduce energy leaks," Misha says.

Sara laughs, "This is going to be a lot of fun. You gals have no idea what you got yourself into. The last time we had damage, we had to contact a company in the neighboring ecosystem and had to sign a lengthy contract. All of it gave me a migraine. I also learned an important lesson then."

"What lesson was that?" Sarang asks with curiosity.

"Well, I am kind of embarrassed, but I agreed to some terms and conditions that were not clearly stated in the contract. I should have trusted my gut that something was fishy, and I went against my instinct. The contractor rushed me to sign and look at the damages in the ecosystem, but I did not discuss it with Xĭlè in advance. It took us a long time to resolve the issues." Sara looks at Xĭlè as she tells the story.

"How did you all resolve this situation in the end?" Misha asks.

"Well, we had to honor some of the unfair terms of the agreement because it was a written contract. However, even if it had been a verbal contract only, Xĭlè would not have wanted to betray her words," Sara says.

"How are the terms unfair?" Misha asks again.

"We had to pay more than 50% of the cost upfront, and that is a lot of money. Their warranty terms were also very stingy, so I believe we got ripped off. I should have consulted with Xĭlè or had someone else double-check the terms before I agreed on our behalf. I would never do that again," Sara has learned her lesson.

"Well, it seems like it's a good lesson learned early on, though. I agree with Xĭlè that we need to honor our agreements. So many people just give lip service. I think speaking truth to power, we should mean what we say, and walk our talk," Misha says.

"Oh totally. We also learned not to assume. We are all complex creatures and sometimes when we say things, we must remember to clarify. ASSUME makes an 'ASS' out of 'U' and 'ME'. We all have different experiences, and our lenses can be so different. Plus, miscommunication occurs when people are not giving grace to each other and just take their own views. If only we could be more understanding and pause before we say things, life would be so much easier," Sara emphasizes.

Sarang listens to the dialogue between Sara and Misha, then, she finally says, "I agree, and thank you for sharing your lessons learned. I try to honor my words, but sometimes I drive myself crazy trying to live up to my promises when they are unreasonable ones. I am thinking now, perhaps we need to take ourselves into account, honoring the words to ourselves and give grace to ourselves."

Who would have thought that Sara's sharing her own embarrassing story would turn into a great bonding moment between Sara, Misha, and Sarang?

MLM* = Micro-Learning Moments

1. Read the fine print before entering into any agreement; the devil's in the details.

2. Do Not ASSUME and, when in doubt, seek clarification.

3. Success or failure, every story can inspire and inform.

4. Cultivate active listening and remember that communication requires all parties to engage, even the quiet ones.

5. Honor your word, even if the agreement does not work out in your favor. This is true integrity.

Chapter 5
Navigating In and Out of Comfort Zones

Xǐlè is looking out over the ecosystem, and she thinks the buildings are looking a bit drab. She wants to spruce them up and have the buildings reflect the creative nature of the ecosystem. Her vision is to help the other inhabitants grow, but how? She recalls how challenging it was for her to come out of her own shell. Toto has done a great job with murals in the past and she wants her to add a few more but she would need assistance. She wants to respect the fact that Toto is an introvert, but she also wants to guide her to be more comfortable with interacting with others. Introverts are usually listeners and observers and have great insights to offer.

As Xĭlè is looking at the walls, Koki slowly swims up. Koki is new to the ecosystem and is still learning how everything works.

"What are you thinking about so intensely?" Koki asks Xĭlè.

"I would like for Toto to paint some murals on these buildings, and I was trying to decide what would look best and who could help her," Xĭlè responds.

"I am willing to help," Koki says and Xĭlè nods.

"Thank you for your willingness to help," she says, "Let me speak to Toto and let her know."

Xĭlè flies to where Toto is quietly working on a painting. Chika, Kia, and Fauna are close by, admiring the painting and chatting amongst themselves.

"Good morning, Toto," Xĭlè says.

Toto puts her paintbrush down. "Do you need something, Xîlé? She feels comfortable enough with Xĭlè to get right to the point.

"I would like some murals on the new buildings, and I would love for you to do them," Xĭlè says.

Toto thinks for a moment.

"I cannot do it right now, but I could start next week. I can think about the design before I begin, and I would need assistance to do such a big project.

28

"We can help," Chika, Kia, and Fauna all chime in.

"Thank you all for volunteering and Koki will help as well. Are you sure you cannot begin until next week? I have some ideas as to what I want," Xǐlè says.

"I have ideas too," Chika says. Chika and Toto have been in the ecosystem for a while, and they feel comfortable having opinions and offering input.

Kia, Fauna, and Koki feel uncomfortable offering their opinions.

"I have to think about it first," Toto says, "Everyone could send me an email with their ideas, and I can sketch out a plan and we can meet next week." She waits a few minutes and goes back to her painting.

Everyone waits for her to say more, but she does not. After a few moments, Xǐlè agrees and tells everyone to email Toto their ideas. The others are surprised that Toto feels so comfortable setting a boundary for herself, but they do not say anything.

Everyone emails their ideas to Toto and on the meeting date, she has several sketches that incorporate ideas from everyone. Toto meekly takes out her sketches, and she feels like she has captured everyone's ideas. However, not everyone is pleased.

"I suggested we add more water features, and I do not think you reflected that idea in your design," Chika exclaims but worries it may upset Toto.

"I included water features, but I guess it can be enlarged. Is that what you mean?" Toto states bluntly.

"It is small, and I was thinking I wanted it on a larger scale," Chika says.

The others do not insert themselves into this dialogue. They just listen and observe. They have some questions, but they do not want things to be uncomfortable, so they are taking a "wait and see" approach.

As Chika and Toto discuss their differences, Xǐlè just listens. Finally, she speaks up.

"Fauna, what do you think?" Xǐlè asks.

Fauna feels very uncomfortable when all eyes are on her.

"I think it's fine," she says, trying to smile away her nervousness.

"How about you Koki?" Xǐlè asks.

"I agree with Chika. I think it needs a larger water feature," he states. Even though it makes him uncomfortable, he wants to give his opinion and be a working part of this project.

"Kia, what do you think?" Xǐlè asks.

"I think that we could add a small creek into the design, and it may do it," she says, trying to be diplomatic.

Everyone is quiet for a moment. Toto is looking at her design very intently.

"I think I could add a creek here," she says and pointed to the top of the sketch.

Everyone studies the sketch and after several minutes they all nod. A creek is the perfect option.

"I will sketch it in, and we can start tomorrow if that works for everyone," Toto says.

Everyone says that it works for them except Kia. She has plans for the next day, but she does not know how to tell everyone. She really wants to help, and she has agreed to be part of this team. When she does not immediately agree, everyone looks at her.

"I made plans in the morning, but I can help in the afternoon," Kia says.

Everyone is quiet and looks at Xǐlè.

"I am proud of you for telling us and honoring the plans that you have already made. I know it can be uncomfortable to say "no" when you are new. Saying "no" is a way of taking care of yourself and setting boundaries. I do want to note that relationships are also about "give" and "take." Be mindful that you do not make everything about you, in a great team, we help each other. Sometimes that means we show each other our vulnerable sides and sometimes we make sacrifices for the sake of advancing the team's position." Xǐlè is careful about her own tone and not making this sound like an intervention or a lecture.

We will see you tomorrow afternoon after your appointment." Kia smiles at Xǐlè. She is proud of herself for speaking up even when it is not easy for her.

The team continues to discuss what is needed for the next day and Xǐlè smiles at their discussions. Everyone is freely expressing their ideas and making plans. Self-care and boundary setting are very important to the mental health of the ecosystem and to the team.

MLM* = Micro-Learning Moments

1. Set clear boundaries for yourself and communicate your expectations. This will help others know what is acceptable and not acceptable.

2. Standing up for yourself can empower you to leave your comfort zone.

3. When you feel uneasy and outside of your comfort zone, lean in.

4. Do not shy away from a new opportunity because of fear.

5. As you grow more comfortable in your roles, remember to connect with others outside of your current network of friends. This will keep you challenging yourself.

Chapter 6
Amplify Your Energy!

Having experienced burnout, Xǐlè wants to ensure that the PeTab ecosystem addresses mental fitness in the most positive light possible. She wants to create a positive environment that helps both the existing and new inhabitants, she thinks that Misha would be great to handle this project. Xǐlè gives a brief overview of her vision, which is to set up an area for yoga and meditation. She visualizes a tranquil spot where the residents may go to chill. Xǐlè also suggests that Misha recruit Sara, Koki, Woodbury, and Luna to assist her.

Misha decides to approach Sara first. Misha's calm presence is the perfect match for Xĭlè's vision for an ecosystem with fulfilled inhabitants. Even though Misha is great at setting boundaries, she can always grow.

"Good morning Sara and Ellie," Misha says.

"Top of the morning to you, Misha. How are you today?" Sara is enthusiastic as always.

"Misha, I appreciate you inviting me to this amplify our energy meeting. I am a techie at heart and not so sure about meditation, but in my line of work, where meeting deadlines is critical, it can be draining." Ellie shrugs her shoulders as she's hanging on the tree trunk.

"Thank you, Sara and Ellie. I am excited. Xĭlè has put me in charge of setting up a yoga and meditation area and I would really like your help," Misha says with a smile.

"That sounds like a great idea, and I would love to assist. The energy of a room is so important, and I can contribute to setting it up in a way to protect outside negativity," Sara advises Misha.

"I second that." Ellie smiles.

"Thank you so much for your willingness to help," Misha says as Koki swims up. When Misha tells Koki what they are doing, he quickly volunteers to offer his services. Koki is very pleased he is included. In his mind, he is imagining how much he can contribute to this meaningful project by utilizing his mad skills as part of a digital generation. Sara and Koki start discussing ideas and Misha observes quietly as she contemplates how to increase engagement from the other folks in the ecosystem.

Koki slowly raises his right hand as Sara continues to talk about her plan of how to arrange this meditation space and does not notice that Koki has questions. Misha takes a quick pause and says, "I think Koki wants to participate. . ."

Koki is relieved that Misha notices his hand is up, and speaks up politely, "Sara and Misha, I am new to all these, but I want to contribute. Not only do we want to protect ourselves from negative energy, I think we should actively illuminate positive energy, right?"

Sara looks perplexed, not sure what Koki is saying.

Misha smiles and interjects, "Care to elaborate?"

Koki gets a little nervous and apologizes, "I don't mean to step on anyone's toes. I just want to clarify. What I meant is protecting ourselves from negative energy seems rather passive. Don't we want to illuminate and spread positive vibes and energy instead?"

Misha thinks for a minute and looks to Sara, and Sara says, "Go ahead, you are welcome to take this one."

Misha proceeds with Sara's permission, "First, you do not have to apologize when you seek clarifications. It is a good practice. We sometimes get lazy in communications, and Xǐlè often says to us that if it weren't for miscommunication, there would be no communication. Xǐlè is generally respectful to everyone, but she is a stickler when it comes to responsiveness. It literally drives her up the wall when we don't respond to her. I think it is because of the environment she used to be in, and it really did a number on her. Xǐlè often says though, timing is everything. You want to be observant and be respectful about other's time."

Sara is working on giving people space and accepting others where they are. It is a work in progress. She has been advised previously that she needs to work on her emotional intelligence and not come across as a bulldozer. Sara listens to the dialogue, thanks Misha and Koki for their input and says, "I was perplexed earlier and almost got intimidated by Koki's questions. I took this as him challenging me and not paying attention to me. I am glad to see how you both interacted and focused on the process of clarification by asking questions. This is done beautifully, I love it."

Misha feels comfortable about leaving Koki, Sara, and Ellie to interact and plan, and she goes ahead to recruit additional teammates from the ecosystems. Misha sees Luna meditating by a tree and gives her a minute to finish her meditation before she approaches her.

"Hello, Misha. Thank you for waiting. Did you need to speak with me?" Luna asks.

"Yes, Xǐlè has put me in charge of creating a yoga and meditation space for the ecosystem, and I invite you to join us as part of the planning committee. Sara and Koki are on board, and they have some creative ideas," Misha says.

"I would love to help. As you know, meditation is an essential part of my practice, and carving out a space to specifically meditate and do some yoga would be a great addition to our ecosystem. I think we should work on building equanimity for our inhabitants," Luna expounds.

Misha puzzlingly asks, "Equa...?"

Luna smiles and says, "Equanimity is calmness under duress. Think of it as a bridge that connects our consciousness to reality. It is the ground for wisdom and freedom and the protector of compassion and love. In its purest form, how do we remain calm when things are going haywire, keeping that stoic presence, you know."

"That's very interesting, but how does one achieve that state?" Misha is curious as this is the question that she studies and achieving that state of mind would be like achieving nirvana.

"Well, that is a life-long learning for some, and I think the key is contentment. I can't wait to collaborate with the team and hear about their ideas," Luna says excitedly.

"Sara, Ellie, and Koki are over by the library. The space next to it is where we want to set up. Would you like to join them while I look for Woodbury?" Misha asks.

"Sure. I will head over to the library and join Sara, Ellie, and Koki," Luna says.

Misha looks and looks and finally finds Woodbury, napping in a hammock. In her mind, she thinks that this is a good sign that he is not busy and would be able to help.

"Woodbury," Misha says, shaking the hammock slightly as she does not want to startle him. When he does not immediately wake up, she shakes it a little harder. Woodbury startles awake.

"Wha-what do you need?" he asks sleepily.

"We are creating a space for yoga and meditation, and we would like your help. Sara, Koki, and Luna are already there discussing ideas," Misha says patiently.

"No," he states and closes his eyes.

Misha stands there dumbfounded, anger bubbling in her stomach. She is tempted to shake his hammock and ask him why he cannot help. Instead, she stands there not speaking a word. Woodbury noticed Misha still standing there. Her silence makes him uncomfortable.

"I just can't," Woodbury answers and this does not improve Misha's mood.

"How about after your nap?" she asks.

"Probably not," he answers and rolls over to sleep.

Misha is normally accepting of everyone, but she is livid inside. She knows that it is better to walk away. If she stays, she will say something that she regrets.

Misha decides to walk away and cool down, and as she approaches the library, Luna notices Misha is not quite herself. Luna pulls Misha aside as she wants to address this in private, whatever the reasons are, "Misha, what happened?" Luna asks calmly.

"Woodbury would rather take a nap than help us," she blurts out.

"I can tell that this has made you angry and understandably so. However, you cannot control Woodbury, but you can control how you respond. You have to protect your energy and control energy leaks. Take deep breaths. C'mon, count with me. Inhale, exhale, and repeat until you calm down," Luna explains to Misha.

Misha nods, fighting her internal turbulence.

"Yes, you have to focus on yourself. The fact is that not everything is about us. Woodbury probably doesn't even understand what he has done," Luna further explains.

"Sometimes we have to be open-minded about others' situations. Even though it can be hard to understand. Remember, equanimity, calmness under duress," Luna says.

"I don't know if I have it in me to practice this, though. I just don't understand," Misha upsettingly says.

"Remember, when Woodbury responds negatively, it is a great test for us to practice kindness. Hurt people hurt people. I don't think he meant it. Perhaps he's working on his own boundary issues. You never know. Xǐlè knew Woodbury for a long time, and I don't think Xǐlè would continue to tolerate someone who could harm the ecosystem. We have to trust our leaders while protecting our own boundaries. That's why Xǐlè appointed you to this project. This is an area that she wants you to grow, ever thought of that?" Luna says.

"I guess you are right, Luna. Let's be the first one to meditate in this room. We should focus on cultivating the right mindset first, physical surroundings is important but reframing our narratives and how we see things is what Xǐlè wants in PeTab, it seems. Xǐlè consulted with me so many times previously that even she is uncomfortable with the various changes going on in our ecosystems, and the diverse views that are sometimes completely opposite from what she believes in. Yet, as the founder of this ecosystem, how she manages change and expectations are critical to the success of this place called, PeTab." Misha says.

"That's right. You know, I heard Koki talking about illuminating positive vibes instead of changing negative vibes and in the short time I spent with Sara and Koki before you returned, I think this is a very special place. There's a great potential for growth, but Xǐlè depends on everyone to behave non-selfishly to help her grow this magical ecosystem." Luna elaborates.

"Luna, I think you may be a better choice for being the person in charge of this project. I don't think I handled my emotions the best and I am slightly embarrassed that I let Xǐlè down." Misha speaks sheepishly.

"Don't be silly. This is not a competition; we are here to grow our ecosystem. We did not know each other, and through challenging situations and understandings, and having each other's back, we grow ourselves and we grow PeTab. That is what Xǐlè wants to do, I am 100% certain." Luna notices that Misha is a bit hard on herself.

"There will be times that I need YOU and others to have my back and be my support system. If we always worry about looking perfect and not showing our vulnerable sides, how do we grow? So, take each lesson as a growth, not mistakes to be erased, but a journey of learning and growth. Cool?" Luna says.

MLM* = Micro-Learning Moments

1. Practice equanimity and calmness under duress; you will gain new insights and experiences if you are calm and see opportunities instead of problems.

2. Meditation is a great way to stay calm. Fifteen minutes every morning helps you refocus your mind and structure your life with intention rather than chaos.

3. When people are upset with us, understand that we have no control over others' behaviors, only how respond to their behaviors.

4. Managing expectations and clearly communicating them with stakeholders are keys to success for leaders.

5. Reward your team according to their individual participation and try not to always make it outcome-dependent. There may be other circumstances that prevent someone from contributing. When in doubt, seek clarifications and do not assume.

Chapter 7
On Boundaries Setting

As Xǐlè reviews the 2nd Quarter Profit & Loss Statement (P&L) of PeTab, she decides to huddle with her confidants. She has some ideas about how to take PeTab to the next level, but she wants input from others before she finalizes her decisions. For the majority of her life, she recognizes that she has been an autocratic leader, well, actually a manager. In the past few years, she recognized that even when she is self-motivated and disciplined, by herself she can only scale PeTab limitedly.

Xĭlè puts a lot of thought into who are the best people to scale PeTab. The ecosystem needs extra funding for items like art supplies, a community garden, and various other projects. They need to utilize the talent within PeTab and start the fundraising efforts.

Kia, Fauna, Gigi, and Toto are chosen because they can collaborate as artists. They would know what supplies are needed and how to make flyers and signs for the fundraiser.

Xĭlè thinks long and hard and wants to include others with meticulous training and coaching experience. She recalls that both Roo and Luna have very impressive professional credentials. After some searches on social media and press releases, she found that both Roo and Luna are on the Advisory Board of the Inner Peace Review (IPR) Board and the Personal Growth Review (PGR) Board. She thinks that would be a perfect blend, Roo is athletic and compassionate, and Luna is intellectual and passionate about learning, these two coaches will be perfect in helping Xĭlè to guide and coach the young inhabitants, she thinks to herself.

Woodbury, Koki, and Alexandra chose to be on the same team. Each has attributes that can add value to this team.

"What should we do to raise money?" Koki asks with a curious tone.

"I think a kayak competition on the river would be the perfect fundraiser for this event," Alexandra says.

"To simplify things, we can have two courses: 101 and 112. 101 is the white-water course and it is a little uncertain, and 112 will involve the calmer water for those who do not know the way of the water." Kia interjects with excitement.

44

"Yes. That way, if they do not like white water, they can choose to do their competitions on the lake. We can include more people that way," Gigi nods.

"How would it work?" Toto asks.

"We can find sponsors for our teams. We can help our sponsors promote their businesses and they can help PeTab grow. Each of these teams can also find something he or she makes and auction it at the event. We can also have bake sales, art sales, and Toto, Chika, and Gigi can showcase their talents. That is a win-win." Fauna says.

"We can even include some art for sale to boost our revenue. What does everyone think?" Alexandra asks. She is excited about all of these ideas.

"I noticed that I may have come across as non-caring and I want to make sure that everyone understands that I have another opportunity, and I have been working very hard toward that goal. I am not someone with too many words, and I feel like I may be estopped because of such misunderstandings. I do have questions regardless about some details. For example, how many animals or kayaks will be in these races? Who would choose the 101 and 112 courses? Would that really bring in money?" Woodbury gathers his courage to speak what's on his mind.

Alexandra looks frustrated. She is proud of her ideas, and she feels like Woodbury is demonstrating inequitable conduct. Before she can respond, Luna steps in. It is obvious that Alexandra's response is not going to be positive.

"I think a kayak competition in the two courses is a great idea. To ensure everyone is included, we can add cycling, putting together a giant puzzle of

PeTab, a treasure hunt, and even a pie-eating contest so it would not be just kayaking," Luna suggests.

Everyone thinks about it and agrees it is a great idea. They will need more planning to have seamless logistics. Woodbury raises some great points. Now they have to make it happen.

Kia, Fauna, and Toto agree to make the flyers and the banners.

"I will also include some of my artwork to be sold. Maybe we could even have an art auction to bring in more money," Toto offers.

"That would be fantastic! Does anyone else have art to include?" Alexandra asks. She feels better now that she has a chance to contemplate others' comments. She knows this is not personal.

"I will create a few paintings," Kia says, and then Fauna chimes in and agrees to make some as well.

Alexandra says she will plan the race, and on the day of the race, she will enlist other volunteers to make it go smoothly. She agrees to create a map and an itinerary as well, using ChatGPT. After all, artificial intelligence, AI, is the hottest topic in all the neighboring ecosystems.

"I can be in charge of the art auction," Woodbury offers.

"I can help with that as well," Kia says.

"The water activities are perfect for me, so I will help with the kayaking events," Koki says.

Fauna agrees to have a booth for the drinks and snacks.

"What kind of snacks do we want?" Fauna asks.

"I think we should have healthy snacks since it is a race and maybe water and drinks to help with hydration," Alexandra suggests, and everyone agrees on that idea.

"We will need help with all the race events and volunteers at every event center," Woodbury adds.

"I will recruit volunteers for that," Alexandra says.

"How and where should we promote the fundraiser?" asks Fauna.

"I can send an email to all the inhabitants of our ecosystem and the neighboring ones, the more the merrier," Luna says.

"You could create a campaign and email everyone our flier, that would save postage costs," Toto says.
"We could also put fliers up all around and have our banners up early. In addition, we need a sponsor form and a form for all the team information," Alexandra says.

"I can create a form for both," Koki says, wanting to be helpful.

"Let's plan out each event so we can include it on the flier," Toto says.

"Maybe the first event should be cycling. This will separate all the teams because everyone goes at different speeds. That way you don't have everyone in a cluster," Alexandra says.

"Next, we could have a puzzle because they will be tired from cycling, and it will give them a little break," Koki says.

"They could pick one member from their team to do the puzzle," Fauna says.

"After they complete the puzzle, the entire team can meet at the river or lake (their choice) for a kayak race. When their entire team has gone the entire distance, they can move on to the treasure hunt," Kia says.

"Great idea," Luna says, "And the treasure hunt could lead them to the pie-eating contest."

"How would that work?" Woodbury warms up as he realizes that everyone accepts his explanation of why he acted so aloof.

"Each animal on the team has to eat a pie without his or her hands before he or she can move on to race to the finish line," Koki says, giggling at the image it gives.

"Hopefully no one throws up on the way to the finish line!" Woodbury says and everyone laughs out loud.

"We need prizes for the winners. Maybe we could set some up for the top two teams," Woodbury says.

"I can get those items donated," Alexandra says.

Xǐlè flies in just as they were finishing the meeting.

"We have created a fundraiser that will be a fun day and raise money," Luna tells Xĭlè.

Xĭlè smiles. She can't wait to hear all of the team's wonderful ideas. Xĭlè is ecstatic that everyone feels so engaged in helping grow PeTab. She recalls a wise thought leader from a neighboring community saying, "Together is better." Xĭlè is working hard to overcome her internal conflict as this is something she created, will it be something she still recognizes after she accepts everyone else's versions of the ecosystems she works so hard to build, or will diversifying experiences and narratives from everyone scale PeTab the way it is meant to be? Only time will tell, Xĭlè thinks to herself.

MLM* = Micro-Learning Moments

1. Leaders should encourage the free flow of ideas and brainstorming, as it is a vital part of planning and initiating new ideas. Not every idea will be adopted but they should be heard.

2. Team Building is key to the overall success of a team.

3. Encouraging everyone to speak up within the team is a great way to unite and motivate a team.

4. Be the last to speak if you want to encourage those within your team to truly share their ideas, you will get more creative ideas that way.

5. A good leader knows how to convert conflicts into learning opportunities.

Chapter 8
On Fear of Missing Out (FOMO) Mindset

Xǐlè is pleased to learn about The Great Race fundraiser the teams came up with. She is proud to see such engagement and creative ideas. She really wants to see everyone take risks, and speak what's on their mind, but in a respectful manner. She is particularly concerned about some of the inhabitants and their "FOMO" mentality. FOMO is Fear of missing out.

The first person she talks to is Chika.

"Good afternoon Chika. How are you today?" Xĭlè asks.

"I am great. How are you?" Chika responds politely as she always does.

"I am doing well. As you know, we have a big race coming up. Would you like to volunteer? There would be a wonderful prize for the winner, and it would help us see any problems we have with the course," Xĭlè says, and she allows Chika a few minutes to think about it.

Chika likes to take calculated risks and does not want to miss out on the prize. It is important to her to please Xĭlè and be a team player. After some thought, she responds.

"I aim to please! I'll be one of the participants," Chika says.

Xĭlè approaches Koki next. She knows he is very involved with the race, and he is proud of his part in putting the course together.

"Koki, I know that you have put a lot into this race, and I want to know if you would like to be one of the select few that tries the course before race day. There would be a wonderful prize for the winner, and it would help us see any problems we have with the course. What do you think?" Xĭlè asks.

Koki is very excited to be one of the first individuals to try the race. He is very comfortable trying new things.

"Yes, I would love to have this opportunity," he responds enthusiastically.

Xĭlè is very pleased with her first two responses. She sincerely hopes that everyone else has a positive reaction. She meets with Toto next.

"Good afternoon, Toto," Xǐlè begins.

"Yes?" Toto responds.

Toto is not big on conversations, but she is a great listener.

Xǐlè decides to just go ahead and ask her if she's interested in trying out the course. It is easier to give her all of the information to process.

"Would you like to be one of the select few that tries the course before race day? There would be a wonderful prize for the winner, and it would help us see any problems we have with the course."

Toto is quiet for a moment, and then replies, "May I have the rest of the day to think about it?" She wants to take time and think about it and maybe talk to her friends Roo and Gigi before she makes a decision.

"Of course," Xǐlè says with a kind smile. She knows that Toto likes to contemplate before making decisions.

Xǐlè sees Paprika and she asks the same questions. They are friends, and Paprika responds, "Thanks for including me, but no thanks. I would be happy to help with other ideas, but let the rest of the team compete."

"You won't feel left out?" Xǐlè says.

"Nope. Why would I? I have enough things on my plate. If I keep saying yes, the quality of my input will suffer." Paprika responds calmly.

Xǐlé smiles as she takes her checklist, next is Kia. She finds Kia and probes her if she wants to try this out.

"Yes, that sounds amazing," Kia says without hesitation. She never wants to miss out on anything. Her answer is normally a resounding yes.

As soon as Kia finishes her YES, she follows up by asking for an opportunity for her childhood friend, Nico. Nico, the tree frog, leaps and trills, with a resounding YES as well. She appreciates Kia looking out for her growth. That's what friends are for.

Next, Roo walks up, and Xǐlè invites her to join. Roo quickly agrees. Roo has lots of energy, and she loves competition. That's a no-brainer.

 Xǐlè approaches Fauna.

"Hello, I hope you are doing well. I wanted to know if you would like to be one of the select few that tries the course before race day. There would be a wonderful prize for the winner, and it would help us see any problems we have with the course," Xǐlè says.

"I am not sure that I want to be part of the race. What would I have to do?" Fauna asks.

Chika hears the conversation along with Alexandra.

"You aren't afraid of missing out?" Chika asks.

"No, I have made my decision. I have other commitments and as much as I hate to miss this, I need to honor my other obligations to my family." Fauna says with a smile.

Alexandra smiles, "I have been afraid of missing out before and have done things that I did not want to do. I have been there and done that, so I understand why you have made your best decision for yourself, Fauna. That shows growth," Alexandra agrees with Fauna.

"Thank you, Alexandra and Chika, for your insight. And thank you, Xǐlè, for the offer. I am going to enjoy watching the games and helping out wherever I am needed," Fauna says.

Toto walks up shortly after, and she tells Xǐlè that she does not want to participate as a competitor. Instead, she will be happy to help as a volunteer to help fill up the water coolers for the competitors during these races.

Xǐlè is proud to witness Toto's growth. In the past, she would have stopped at "No." She is a zebra with few words...

Now Xǐlè recognizes that planning such races will take lots of effort and detailed planning. However, she is thrilled that each of the inhabitants has grown so much both in their skill sets and emotional maturation. FOMO or not, this team will elevate to great heights as they watch out for each other. She has no questions about that!

MLM* = Micro-Learning Moments

1. Don't allow the fear of missing out to sway you from your priority. Be focused and intentional when pursuing your dreams!

2. People will respect you when your words and actions are congruent with your values.

3. Being a team player sometimes means supporting rather than controlling.

4. Make choices for you based on your inner compass and don't outsource your self-worth based on others' opinions of you.

5. Once you agree to participate, give it your best shot.

Chapter 9
Value Your Truth

It is race day and everyone is both excited and nervous. The teams have been chosen and everyone is saying that they are going to win. It is all for a good cause after all, so win or lose, it is a win for the ecosystem.

The first team calls themselves, "The Mavericks." On this team are Sara, Chika, Luminary, Alexandra, Mia, Ellie, and Hetter. Xǐlè will oversee as she's the protector of the group.

"The Mavericks are going to win!" Sara yells, getting her team pumped up to race.

Everyone on her team agrees with Sara and they cheer.

The second team dubs themselves the "Zen Crew" and it consists of Misha, Paprika, Sarang, and Roo.

"Let's all have a moment of meditation so we can focus on this journey," Misha says and they all close their eyes and murmur quietly.

The third team says they are the "Novelists" and on their team is Scar, Timo, Woodbury, Keola and Hanso.

"We will do whatever we have to do so we can win!" Scar says and he smirks at the other teams. Everyone is concerned by his words, but they are trying to be positive.

Coming in on the fourth and final team are Kia, Gigi, Toto, Koki Fauna, and Nico. They say they are the "The Truth Seekers."

"A race, ha, challenge accepted." The Truth Seekers yell in unison.

Xǐlè and Peanut are running the games with some volunteers from another ecosystem. They invite the chameleon. This panel of three judges remains neutral as their main objective is to keep everyone safe and to raise funds to grow the ecosystem.

The first event is cycling, and each team has chosen to put certain members in this event. Chika is cycling for her team. Her teammates are cheering her on. The second team has chosen Misha as their cyclist. Scar volunteers for his team and the sneer on his face tells everyone he is going to bend the rules a bit. Last but not least, Keola is chosen from her group. The race begins and it is clear that Scar is going to use every nasty trick to win. He takes shortcuts, kicks up dirt in everyone's face, and spins his tires so that rocks fly into his competitors. He wins but even his team does not look happy about it. Peanut gives everyone water because they look hot and frustrated. She wants to do her part.

The puzzle is next and Scar tags in Timo to complete the puzzle. Scar has given Timo a lead, but he is so frustrated because he knows Scar didn't play a fair game that he falls behind. Toto comes in and beats him on the puzzle. She tags in Koki for the kayaking, just as the other two teams arrive and start their puzzle. Timo is still discombobulated by Scar and the puzzle is hard for him.

Koki picks up his kayak and Fauna tells him the guidelines. Koki quickly picks up the paddle and starts his race. It isn't long before she hears HansSolo behind her. Timo must have finished his puzzle. She can hear the others, Paprika and Kia coming as well. Hanso passes him at the last moment and takes the lead. Koki comes in a close second and the others follow shortly after. Everyone is involved in the treasure hunt. Luna gives everyone a map and wishes them luck.

Everyone tries to follow the clues and find the treasure but, in the end, The Novelists find the golden coin below the waterfall. The others are sad, but they know there is one event left and they still have a chance. The Pie Eating Contest.

Everyone is participating and when your entire team eats their pie then your team will win. The Novelists receive a one-minute advantage for winning the most events. They begin eating and the others follow when the time is up. Sara quickly polishes off her pie and then she waits for her team to finish. Timo finishes his pie next, followed by Misha, and then Woodbury, Scar, and Keola finish. The Novelists complete the challenge first and win the first race in the ecosystem. Everyone congratulates them and is a good sport. Xǐlè hands out trophies and makes a speech.

"Congratulations The Novelists on your win. Everyone did a great job today, even though some people did not always play as a team. Sometimes self-interest is okay, but we must remember that selfishness is not acceptable in the ecosystem. Sometimes the people who start with you on the journey will not finish with you. They have other plans and so do you. Serendipity happens more than you think, let it be!"

"What is Serendipity?" Luna asks.

"An unplanned fortunate discovery," Xǐlè says.

"You're right! It does happen more than we think. Besides, I like the word." Luna says and everyone laughs.

It has been a successful race and they have raised lots of money for the ecosystem. Xǐlè believes in everyone's potential but sometimes is shocked by their true capabilities. She knows that it is important to draw boundaries and work at not only creating those boundaries, but we have to pay attention to what we allow in order to thrive. She knows that Scar has not been a good sport and that is his truth. He might survive but he would never thrive with that mentality. But you have to "let them" and stop being an enabler. He will eventually have to take responsibility for his actions. Sometimes we have to stay back and let them do things that we do not condone because it is not our journey. As much as we want to point out the error of their ways it is not our place. It is their path, and we have to create our own path and not worry so much about the paths of others. It will make our race go smoother and, in the long run, we will be happier for it. Run your race, the best you can, and stop focusing on what others are doing. They will get you off of your path and will hinder the race that you want to run. Worry about yourself and what you need to be doing.

Everyone has their truth, you have to value their truth, even if you don't agree with it.

MLM* = Micro-Learning Moments

1. Those who take short cuts do not win in the long run.

2. Choose right over convenience.

3. The Chinese have a saying, "It takes a hundred lies to cover one lie." The truth will come out eventually, be upfront about it. You gain more respect that way.

4. Recognize that our truth is not the same as others as we all have different experiences and narratives. Respect the differences and learn from them.

5. It is best to let others learn the lessons for themselves.

Chapter 10
Collaboration and Competitiveness Reinterpreted

Xĭlè has scheduled a meeting by the waterfall to reflect on the race with the inhabitants of the ecosystem. Everyone is with the team they are in for the race. Xĭlè has heard from several inhabitants that they are leaving, and she wants to discuss that first. She has heard whispers around the ecosystem, and she wants to clear up all the rumors.

"Good morning everyone. Thank you for coming and for making the race such a success. I am happy that we had that time together as some of our inhabitants will be leaving. Woodbury, Hanso, Hanrietta, and Keoli have decided that they need to leave our ecosystem. They wish to pursue something that is more aligned with their own values. Remember, sometimes the people who start on our journey will not finish with us." Xǐlè says and everyone looks at the group that is leaving. They are sad but they understand that everyone has to live their own journey.

"It is OK. We have to give them our blessings. It is fate that we became part of a team, there are lessons for each of us to learn and these lessons will help us grow in life. Hopefully, these lessons are more positive than negative, but in the end, even with each fall, we grow. " Xǐlè says as she tries to hold her tears back.

Luminary speaks up and adds that she has to leave as well.

"I am sorry guys, but I am leaving too," Luminary says a bit sadly. However, she and Xǐlè will always be friends. She just feels that her purpose is somewhere else. It is apparent that this makes Xǐlè sad, but she understands. Sometimes people outgrow the ecosystem, and sometimes our ecosystem outgrows them. She has to seek fulfillment elsewhere.

"Is anyone else leaving?' Alexandra asks.

Everyone is quiet.

Mia, the octopus wiggles out of the aquarium with his eight flexible arms and dances across the floor. He then raises three of his arms, "I know I have not participated much, it's kinda messy for me to control all my arms. I am a big fan of our ecosystem, and I will stay to help Xǐlè and all of you with what I can. You all are family to me; I am here to defend my friends. Just say the word."

"Good. For a moment there I thought we were not going to have an ecosystem." Alexandra says with a sigh of relief. I am here to stay, as I have grown to be fond of this place and I know Xĭlè can be preachy sometimes, but she really cares about us. That is why she can be harsh at times. She wants to prepare us for the outside world.

Hetter, Toto, Gigi, and Nico all raise their hands, "We are here for now until we figure out what we are meant to be."

"Everyone, including the water dwellers, can enjoy the fruits of our labor. It has been difficult at times to bring others into our ecosystem. Expansion creates chaos, and people have to sometimes have hard conversations to achieve TRUE DEIA in the ecosystem." Xĭlè says and many of the original inhabitants agree.

"Honestly, there were times I just wanted all the new inhabitants to go somewhere else," Sara says. She is not afraid to speak her truth.

"Sara, I admire you for speaking your truth. I have to explore my spiritual side and examine potential energy leaks, so I don't get frustrated. Thank goodness we have Luna here; she saved my bacon several times." Misha says to Sara.

Sarang normally does not speak up, but she says, "I am learning to say "no" and in the end, I know that people will respect me more for saying it." Sarang says quietly and Xĭlè smiles. She loved seeing growth in her inhabitants. "I am here to stay as I don't want to see Xĭlè being taken advantage of. Xĭlè and I had several talks about what will help me be fulfilled, and she understands that if I have to part, our friendship trumps our work at the village. I trust her vision and whatever it takes for me to help, I will be here."

"I am here to stay too. I feel accepted here and I just want to draw. That is my calling and until I reach the next portion of my journey. I believe Xǐlè could use my help." Toto says with confidence that no one else has witnessed before.

"Henrietta is also leaving. She indicates that she's a short-timer and she has other goals in life. We wish her well." Xǐlè says.

"When people are toxic, we cannot just throw them out of our ecosystems. We offer chances, and we have to be fair, especially with others who hold different backgrounds and values than us. We must also adapt and grow so that we can examine what is making them toxic, and not tiptoe around. We do have to treat everyone as individuals but with sensitivity. That may sound mushy, and it can be an incredibly frustrating experience, but true diversity, equity, and inclusion is not only lip service. It is important that we all learn to live together." Xǐlè says, glancing at Sara.

"I know that everyone is not happy about the way I ran the race yesterday." Scar says. Everyone nods.

"If it was left up to some people, I know I would be out of here," he says looking at Sara.

"But I appreciate the fact that we can have this candid conversation and I hope to stay and grow with you all." Scar says.

"When you know better, you do better," Sarang says quietly. Xǐlè smiles and she is proud of her for speaking up.

"I agree. You know better now," Luna says.

'I do and I will try hard not to disappoint everyone too," Scar says.

"Our goal is for everyone to live their lives with fulfillment and be happy. Work is work, and we are all on this earth in a very short time, why play games with one another when we can help each other grow?" Xǐlè says.

Everyone agrees, even Sara.

PeTab has come together and is thriving because the inhabitants work together for one common goal. Even though everyone has different values and opinions, they all agree that they are better together. Working as a team is going to make our ecosystem thrive for many years to come.

In the future, we will have new challenges. We will continue to expand and to grow. With growth comes change and that can be difficult for those that have been at the ecosystem from the beginning but, with Xǐlè's guidance, they will make it through any trials and tribulations that they encounter.

Having healthy competition can be very great, and sometimes it is necessary. In the end, though, collaboration makes us stronger, as a team and a community. There's no "I" in team...

"PeTab has so many talents and each grows exponentially by the minute. Even Scar admits his own flaws and seeks to grow, that is the power of our team. While some may think that a team strengthens when we witness each other's strengths, I think a team strengthens when we help each other grow out of our vulnerabilities." Xǐlè says.

"We should have a race every year and add events. Maybe we could compete against neighboring ecosystems and seek additional corporate funding to grow PeTab. Of course, we would win!" Sara says and everyone cheers.

"I love your enthusiasm." Xǐlè giggles.

"I agree with Sara, we would win!" Scar says and everyone is happy that he would be on their team. Even if they do not like his methods with them, maybe he is reformed, and they could be a positive influence on him.

"I will be watching you Scar!" Timo says and everyone laughs, including Scar, which is rare.

"Next year we have more time for planning, and we know where we made mistakes. I know we can make it better. I can also start making flyers early so they can be really nice." Toto says and Xǐlè is extremely happy that she is finding her voice in the ecosystem.

"It is agreed that we will do the race next year and we will make it grand and collaborate more with neighboring habitats. We will earn even more money and it will be fun to meet new people and see how their habitat works." Xǐlè says.

Everyone has a nice picnic beneath the waterfall and talks about the next race. Hearing all the ideas and seeing everyone working together makes Xǐlè extremely happy. Xǐlè requests a picture to show the team's unity before everyone heads home. After all, she created all of this... She just does not know what is next. Whatever it is, it will never be dull for certain.

Unity is strength...
when there is teamwork and collaboration, wonderful things can be achieved.

- Mattie Stepanek

MLM* = Micro-Learning Moments

1. Collaboration creates ecosystems that emphasize unity instead of competition.

2. Competition is not always bad, healthy competition promotes personal growth and creativity.

3. Fostering collaboration between team members should be one of the primary goals a servant leader strives for.

4. Collaboration allows team members to feel seen and be heard.

5. As a leader, take pride in the environment you have created through encouragement, attention, and collaboration.

Appendix A: Level Up Readings and Podcasts

Acuff, Jon. *Finish: Give Yourself the Gift of Done*. Penguin USA, 2018.
---. *Soundtracks*. Baker Books, 6 Apr. 2021.

Braun, Randi. *Something Major: The New Playbook for Women at Work*. New Degree Press, 1 Mar. 2023.

Brooks, Arthur. *FROM STRENGTH to STRENGTH: Finding Success, Happiness, and Deep Purpose in the Second Half... Of Life*. S.L., Portfolio Penguin, 2021.

Brooks, Arthur C, and Oprah Winfrey. *Build the Life You Want*. Penguin, 12 Sept. 2023.

Brown, Brené. *The Gifts of Imperfection*. Hazelden Publishing, 2022.

---. *Atlas of the Heart*. New York Random House, 2021.

---. *Rising Strong : How the Ability to Reset Transforms the Way We Live, Love, Parent, and Lead*. New York, Random House, 2017.

--- . *A Concise Summary of Brené Brown's Daring Greatly ... In 30 Minutes*. Garamond Press, 2012.

Sheena Yap Chan. *The Tao of Self-Confidence*. John Wiley & Sons, 23 May 2023.

Cheung, Ashley. *Building a Leadership Habitat*. Barnes and Nobles Press, 2022.

Clear, James. *Atomic Habits : Tiny Changes, Remarkable Results : An Easy & Proven Way to Build Good Habits & Break Bad Ones*. New York, Avery, An Imprint Of Penguin Random House, 2018.

Dalio, Ray. *Principles: Life and Work*. New York, Simon And Schuster, 2017.

Duckworth, Angela. *Grit: The Power of Passion and Perseverance*. New York Scribner, 2016.

Natasha Craig Durkins. *Fiercely Joyful*. New Degree Press, 31 Oct. 2023.

Elmore, Tim. *A New Kind of Diversity*. Simon and Schuster, 25 Oct. 2022.

Gable, Lisa. *Turnaround: How to Change Course When Things Are Going South*. Ideapress Publishing, 3 Oct. 2021.

Grant, Adam M. *Hidden Potential The Science of Achieving Greater Things*. Random House, Oct. 2023.

---. *Think Again : The Power of Knowing What You Don't Know*. London, Wh Allen, 2021.

---. *Give and Take : A Revolutionary Approach to Success*. London, Phoenix / Orion Books, 2013.

Green, Mark E. *Activators : A CEO's Guide to Clearer Thinking and Getting Things Done*. United States, Mark E. Green, 2018.

Hadeed, Kristen, and Simon Sinek. *Permission to Screw up : How I Learned to Lead by Doing (Almost) Everything Wrong*. New York, New York, Portfolio/Penguin, 2017.

Maxwell, John C. *Developing the Leader within You*. Nashville, Tennessee Nelson Books, 2018.

---. *The 21 Irrefutable Laws of Leadership*. Nashville, Tenn., Thomas Nelson ; London, 2008.

---. *The Five Levels of Leadership: Proven Steps to Maximize Your Potential*. New York, Center Street, 2021.

Raz, Guy. *HOW I BUILT THIS SIGNED EDITION : The Unexpected Paths to Success from the World's Most Inspiring Entrepreneurs.* Boston, Houghton Mifflin Harcourt, 2020.

Raz, Guy, and Nils Parker. *How I Built This : The Unexpected Paths to Success from the World's Most Inspiring Entrepreneurs.* Boston, Houghton Mifflin Harcourt, 2020.

Scott, Kim. *RADICAL CANDOR : How to Get What You Want by Saying What You Mean.* S.L., Pan Books, 2019.

---. *Radical Candor: Fully Revised & Updated Edition.* St. Martin's Press, 1 Oct. 2019.

Shetty, Jay. *Think like a Monk : Train Your Mind for Peace and Purpose Every Day.* New York, Simon & Schuster, 2020.

Sinek, Simon. *Leaders Eat Last.* London, United Kingdom, Portfolio Penguin, 2014.

---. *Start with Why: How Great Leaders Inspire Everyone to Take Action.* London, Penguin, 2009.

---. *The Infinite Game.* London, Uk, Penguin Business, 2019.

Sinek, Simon, and Ethan M Aldridge. *Together Is Better : A Little Book of Inspiration.* New York, New York, Portfolio/Penguin, 2016.

Sun, Lisa. *Gravitas.* Hay House, Inc, 12 Sept. 2023.

Van Edwards, Vanessa. *Captivate : The Science of Succeeding with People*. London, Portfolio Penguin, 2018.

---. *Cues : Master the Secret Language of Charismatic Communication*. New York, Portfolio, 2022.

Yusim, Anna. *Fulfilled : How the Science of Spirituality Can Help You Live a Happier, More Meaningful Life*. New York, Grand Central Life & Style, 2017.

Podcast Recommendations

Godin, S. (Host). (2012-2013). Seth Godin's Startup School. Earwolf & Seth Godin. https://seth-godins-startup-school.simplecast.com/.

Grant, A. (Host). (2021-present). ReThinking with Adam Grant. TED. https://adamgrant.net/podcasts/rethinking/

Grant, A. (Host). (2018-present). Work Life with Adam Grant. TED. https://adamgrant.net/podcasts/work-life/.

Maxwell, J. (Host). (2018-present). Maxwell Leadership Podcast. https://johnmaxwellleadershippodcast.com/.

Mylett, E. (Host). (2016-present). The Ed Mylett Show. Ed Mylett. https://www.edmylett.com/podcast.

Raz, G. (Host). (2016-present). How I Built This with Guy Raz. Guy Raz & Wondry. https://www.guyraz.com/howibuiltthisbook.

Shetty, J. (Host). (2016-present). On Purpose with Jay Shetty. iHeartPodcasts. https://jayshetty.me/podcast/.

Sinek, S. (Host). (2020-present). A Bit of Optimism. Simon Sinek. https://simonsinek.com/podcast/.

Virtual Water Cooler Chat. (2023-present). Virtual Patent Gateway. https://www.vpgateway.com/podcasts

 Notes

 Notes

 Notes

 Notes

 Notes

 Notes

Notes

Notes

 Notes

 Notes

 Notes

 Notes

 Notes

 Notes

 Notes

 Notes

 Notes

 Notes

 Notes

 Notes

 Notes

 Notes

ISBN 979-8-8653-2602-1

Made in the USA
Columbia, SC
06 September 2024